# The Melody of a Broken Heart

By Lunar Patni

To Loki, Wil,
The Pirates, Braxton, Mrs.Wilson,
and Sra.Vidal

To the memories of Z, Abby, and
Elliot.

PART ONE

# Her.

She stomps up the steps
I descend slowly
She wears light blue puppies
I drape myself in sage predators
She walks on the left
I walk on the right
And I'm over her,
I really am.
But I'm not over our memories.
We make eye contact
And for a second, I miss her
Especially when I see the slight
nostalgia glistening in her eyes.
But then she reverts to her ugly
sneer and I remember everything.
I don't feel bad anymore
But something hurts every time.
Every time I see her without me
And I have to pretend to brush her
off
But she doesn't look happy.
She misses me, I know it.
And of course, I miss her
But that won't change her
And neither can I.

Until the end of time, I will
always have feelings for you.
Not always good.
Not necessarily bad.
But I'll always have them
And they'll always be for you.

# Not again

A 26-year-old man attempted to
groom me.
This is not the first time this
has happened.
My only question is
Why can't people love me like
people twice my age do?
Do they also have double the love
they can give?
Should I wait?
Or is getting groomed again my
only option

# Mature

I was 11
He was 17
11.
I was supposed to be outside
Out with friends
Drinking apple juice
Playing hopscotch
But instead, I was inside
Being unloved
Getting groomed
"You're so mature for your age."

# Loved

When I say her name
Even if I'm not talking about her
I shudder
And I remember every heartbreak
she caused
And my heart still breaks in two
When will this stop?
Will this stop?
I desperately want to forget her
She doesn't deserve my tears
I miss her
I love her
No.
I love**d** her.

# Dead

She's a different person now
Not the girl I loved
not my best friend
My best friend is gone
Dead.
She's dead.
Get it in your head.
She's dead
And someone else replaced her.

# Sixteen.

Maybe I was a bad person
Maybe I manipulate people with a
lack of awareness
Maybe I'm mean
And violent
And horrible
And aggressive
And I don't know how to act
Or maybe I'm a teenager.
Maybe I'm still figuring out life
My personality
myself.
Maybe you're right about me
And maybe I'm a good-for-nothing
bully
Or maybe
Just maybe
I'm sixteen.

## Sober

One day
Two day
Three day
Four.
Five day
Six day
Sober no more.
Seven day
Eight day
Nine day
Ten
Will this heartbreak ever end?
One day
Two day
Three day
Four.
Five day
Six day
Back on the floor.

When I am yelled at, I think deep
in my mind
I cut right to left
The skin jiggles
And bounces back
And splits open.
I can see the skin turn ivory
And small ruby beads start to form
I shudder.
My body twitches,
Shakes,
AndIi look away
And I ignore it.

## My Favorite Song

When someone asks me what my
favorite song is
I don't think of words put to a
rhythmic beat
I think of you.
I walk to the steady beat of your
heart
I hum your breath
I sing your words
You are my favorite song
On repeat
Every day

# Left to right

When I cut myself, I refuse to cut
left to right.
I'll cut right to left
Up to down
Down to up
But never left to right
Because left to right is the way I
read
And I'll be damned if cutting
takes away another joy of mine
When it has already taken so much
away from me

Crayons

My parents gave me caramel paper
when I was very young, but no
utensils seemed to work on it
When I was at the ripe age of
eleven I was introduced to magical
crayons. These were silver crayons
that could write on my caramel
paper.
So I scribbled and drew designs on
my paper
And to my joy (and slight regret)
I found the silver crayons had
turned my paper red.
Little ruby beads spilled out of
my paper, rivers of wine pouring
out.
It was exhilarating
I had never experienced anything
quite like it before
SoIi kept drawing on my paper
And watching my magical silver
crayons
Turn my caramel paper the color of
a cardinal

## Walk of Shame

An alarm clock blares in my
stomach
Hiccups plague my throat
Its time
And I know it.
I raise a shaky hand and excuse
myself
I trudge my tired body to the
restroom
I kneel in front of the toilet
I contemplate
Then stick two fingers down my
throat
Acid builds up and falls into the
bowl
I gag
Coughs echo in the stalls
Finally, chewed-up pieces of food
cascade out of my mouth
A garbage waterfall
My eyes tear up
I wash my hands to rid them of
acid
I take a quick look in the mirror
A miserable wannabe boy looks back
at me

I keep my head down and walk back
to class
My throat burns
My sleeve is wet
But life continues as usual

When I see a boy whose leg is
trembling
Or a girl who is breathing too
fast
I wonder
"What would it take to make me man
up and hug them?"

## Archetype

I am a Writer.
I am supposed to write every
waking hour of my life,
writing should **be** my life.
And it is
But I'm no good at it
My writing is comparable to a
typewriter
It can be used to create new work
But it is old
And outdated
And unneeded.

I am a Lover
Romance is my life
I love and love and love
But to no avail
I'm no good at loving either
My love is one-sided.
My love is calling his phone and
leaving a note sweet enough to get
cavities and not getting a
response
Pathetic.

I am a Villain

I am evil
I don't do it on purpose
And don't want to be evil
But I am.
I am rage
I am revenge
AndIi am pettiness
And I am guilty.
I believe those who wrong me
should be wronged
ThereforeIi am evil
And manipulative
And predetermined for hell.

I am a Writer
I am a Lover
I am a Villain

And I am not good at any of it.

## Over my Shoulder

I sit up straight
And try to look pretty
Just in case someone is watching
me from afar
Maybe they'd be reading over my
shoulder
Maybe even watching me type this.
Someone might watch when I switch
my music and think to themself "I
love that song!"
Someone could be noticing every
little detail about me
HowIi crack my fingers or bite my
pen when get nervous
How I doodle and scribble on paper
and my hands
They would notice the scars on my
arm
And wish to kiss each one
But I'm scared of them
And they might be scared of me
So we'll never speak
And they'll sit and watch me
Or not

Maybe I'm just typing all this with a delusional tumor in my head.

# Writer's Block

I have no thoughts in my brain
I need to write
I need to publish
I need to get these damned
thoughts out of my head
But I can't think of the words to
describe my tragedies.
Tragedies.
Are they even really tragedies?
I want to write, I have to write
But I'm stuck
My brain is blank.
A white space in my head with no
words flying around.

# Lightbulb

I need ideas
So I think and think and think
And just as it seems like it's to
no avail
I have an idea
DING!
A lightbulb appears over my head
I stare in shock
This never happens to me
I reach up to hold it
AndIi am burned
Burnt by my own idea
So I wear gloves to protect myself
from my thoughts
I reach up and the bulb shatters
Glass falls in my eyes and pricks
my skin
Each shard gives me a short new
idea
As much as it pains me, I must
continue
Creativity is pain.

# Writing is Pain

Beauty is pain
To be beautiful you must go
through a checklist
I will not expose this checklist
because, as you can tell with a
quick look at me, I do not know
it.
So instead I will talk about my
writing
As always.
I bleed onto my papers and use
incarcerated livers to donate
ideas to me
My fingers grow tired and dance
themselves to the bone while
gripping the pen
My brain is the equivalent of a
bucket with a hole in it
Even if I do have an idea it'll
fall out before I can grab it.
Writing is pain
And it's even more painful when
you're bad at it.

I love you


I love you like the sun loves the
moon
Eternally, but too far away.
I love you like a boy watches his
crush
With caution and worship.
I love you like the stars love the
sky
With brightness, hope, and nursing
I love you like a piano loves to
duet with a violin
With harmony and love that
contrasts like a puzzle piece
I love you like

Harmony

I am a melody
The beat of my heart
The scratches of my nails
The running of my blood
The sound of my steps
Clack
Clack
Clacking through the halls
When the sound of my song flows
through your existence
You stand in shock
You take a sharp blade
And you saw off your ears.
You can't bear to be without me,
right?
But you can't be with me either
You can't decide
So you cut off your ears so you
don't have to.

# Good Dog

I'm a good dog
I'll wait for you for hours on end
Fur scruffed up
Nails untrimmed
My stomach growls
But I don't mind
I'm a good dog
So I'll keep quiet
Though some food would be nice.
When you finally come home my tail
wags
I missed you!
I'm a hungry dog
A whiny dog
But I'm still a good boy
Right?
I close my eyes
But when I pry them open again I
don't see you
I'm alone in a gray cell
No friends
No family
No one to love
I thought I was a good dog?

# Overdose

Fifteen hundred milligrams of
paracetamol ran through my
bloodstream.
My head hurts
I feel regret
I quickly stick two fingers down
my throat and lean over the bowl
of the toilet.
I gag and feel something stab at
my throat
Red spills out of my mouth
Not scarlet or crimson
Nor cardinal intestines
Just red.
I continue
Acid coats my fingers
God.
What's wrong with me?
Barely an overdose
Average teenage "girl"
Everyone experiments with suicide
I don't want to be alive.

# Bloody Jellyfish

My legs sting
I don't think I can walk
My thigh scratches
The only thing that will ever
touch me intimately is this bloody
bandage
God, it pains me.
It stings like a bloody jellyfish
attacking my thigh
**FUCK.**
I'm limping.
Part of me hopes, and prays, that
someone will notice
I want someone to notice or care
Caress my thigh and reassure me
I want you to tell me I'm okay and
kiss my scars
I want you to ask me if I'm okay
with what you're doing and make
sure I'm comfortable
Calm me down
Don't try to move your lips up
higher on my thigh
Don't be sexual, please
Keep me calm and safe, please
Help me.

## Pinocchio

I received a new name days ago
It stays now and it'll stay in the
morrow
Pinocchio.
My nose is so large, so
unreasonably mountainous, that I'm
called Pinocchio.
Does that mean I'm a real boy?
Not yet.
Anti-Semitic cries reach my ears
They ask me where my yarmulka is
I'm Muslim.
People pretend to hail Hitler to
eradicate me
I didn't do anything
"Terroristic Pinocchio's gonna
bomb the school!"
I wish I could chop it off.

I overdosed.
Read 9:23 pm.

## Rotten Apple

I'm not a good person
I know that
I want to change
I want to rid myself of red-hot
anger and ugly hatred
Im a bag of apples
Rotten
Thrown away
Bruised and battered
But I'm not a victim
Don't call me that.
I'm a bad apple
I am a shit person
I know that
I deserve the threats and insults
receive every day
Strike me down God, I pray, Kill
me!
I don't deserve to live
Strike me down
Throw away the bad apple
The scum of the earth

# Below Average

I am below average.
Height - below average.
Looks - below average.
Grades - below average.
Love life - below average.
Talent - below average.
Friends - below average.
Success - below average.
Charisma - below average.

Weight - above average.
Problems - above average.
Illnesses - above average.
Scars - above average.

Will to live - N/A

# Sophia

Sophia's dead
I can't be her anymore
A little girl in a pink tutu
Surrounded by parental love
I'm not sophia
I'm not the girl who was almost
raped
I'm the boy, no, a boy
I'm just a boy living life
I'm not a female victim

# Ghost

My boyfriend is a ghost
He's cold
rarely speaks
And only comes out at night
He lets me love him
And he pretends to love me
Not well.
He's a bad actor
I can't touch him
I feel alone when I'm with him
My boyfriend is a ghost
So maybe, just maybe, I could die.
If Iie I'll be with him
We can be ghosts together

# Pretty Boy

Mint hair envelops my thoughts
Thoughts of me
Thoughts of you
I hope violet thoughts cascade in
your dreams
A dream of you
A dream of me
When you call me your pretty boy,
I feel like a fraud
How could someone so beautiful
look up at someone like me?
It's as if a dove were to look up
at a raven
A raven is an acquired taste
A dove is beloved.
I feel broken
Like I'm lying to you
Why else would you think I'm so
pretty?
But I don't want it to stop.
So you're my darling
And I'm your pretty boy.

## Ash

Mint hair swirls in my thoughts
I hope violet locks dance in yours
Wait...
I think I've told this story
before.
Your small freckles are permanent
craters on my brain
I miss you.
This used to be a love poem
Not anymore
It has enveloped itself into a
cocoon and changed
It has adapted
As have I.
You don't love me anymore
But that's okay
I expected this
This isn't unusual
It's like my love life is a
weather forecast
Storms and ghosting ahead
Sunny days have yet to come.

# Imagine

I'm tossing and turning
And ever so yearning
For you to be by my side.
I hold my pillow
I hold my breath
And turn the lights down low.
I shut my eyes
But for once I don't cry
Instead, I start to lie
I lie to myself that you are right
there
Your smile beaming in the night.
It shines so bright it steals the
light
And it is light once again.
But of course, it's all a dream
A dream I wish were true
So I sit there yearning
My heart, she is burning,
As I wait for only you.

Absence makes the heart grow
fonder

Is that why you blocked me?

# Satan

Satan is not a little red man with
a pointy tail and a pitchfork.
She is a dirty blonde, sometimes a
brunette girl with pale yet
somehow tanned skin wearing
practically nothing.
She doesn't throw punches, she
hisses into others' ears with her
snakish tongue until your life is
ruined
Shell gossip and spread lies about
you until all your friends drop
like flies
You catch more flies with honey
than vinegar, so why do her
sadistic bloody rituals attract so
many?
Satan gets validation by
sexualizing herself and throwing
her body at every other man who
walks past.
Satan is broken in the head and
she has no heart but she doesn't
care
Satan deserves Hell and more

She walks among us but when you
point her out she reverts back to
her seemingly innocent self
You can't catch her
You can't touch her
(unless you're taking her clothes
off, that is)
Sure, she's just a child,
Sure she's my age,
But she knows what she's doing
She loves to ruin lives, I swear
she gets some sort of sick
sadistic pleasure out of it.
Satan is a teenage girl with a
tongue of snakes and knowledge
about you that you don't even know
about yourself.
Satan is not a baby with a sharp
fork.
She is so
SO
So much more than that.

# Jellyfish

Long swirly tendons fly in the
water
Each strand has its own nerve
endings
Each strand is laced with venom
But why antagonize Jellyfish if
humans are the same way?
Our hands are laced with venom
Our voices are coated in poison.
Jellyfish lash out for defense
Humans sting for sadist fantasies.
Don't antagonize jellyfish,
Who sting in defense.
Antagonize the humans,
Who does harm for fun?

Poison and Venom

Our words are poison, for you need
to ingest them for them to do
damage

Our fists are venom, for they can
hurt just by touch.

I don't spread my legs
I spread my heart
And sometimes I spread it too
thin.

## My Writing has hit Puberty

After publishing my first book, my
writing has changed.
Not by much,
But if you really look into it
There are subtle differences
A different connotation to the
words
Words such as river have tuned to
lakes
For a river can rage
But a pond is calm.
Writing has taken a thin needle
and has extracted my anger
Of course, it still returns
sometimes
But my writing has matured
And so have I.

The blind see without eyes
The deaf hear without ears
The mute speak without a voice
I love without a heart

He is the beauty of my poems
He is the essence of perfection
I am the cold autumn air
And he is the warmth you feel when
you step out of the shade
And into the sunlight
He *is* my poetry.
All I do is take a butterfly net
And I chase his beauty around
And I capture it
And turn them into words
And write them down.

I am not a villain.
I am a rose with thorns
And you are the only one smart
enough to wear gloves.

# Bullseye

A drawing has been procured of me
But it doesn't look like me.
In the drawing, I am pictured with
large sagging breasts
I am shown with a mountainous nose
And people tell me it's not a big
deal
But I want to cry.
I want to cry and sob and scream
I want to yell and kick something,
someone, anything.
Anger coats my every waking
thought
I feel hot
Im ugly, yes, I know
But am I so ugly you must draw me
so disfigured?
I shatter every time I hear that
something like this has happened
once again
I suppose I must be a target
Bullseye.

# Brisbane

Ten thousand miles away in
Brisbane
A grave was filled with seemingly
nothing
In the grave is an old rosewood
coffin that is surprisingly ornate
Small dust particles swim in the
air of the coffin
My soul rests here.

# Break up no.3

Love is all I chase in this life
and yet here I am
Denied it yet again.
Damn it, you were supposed to love
me!
I dreamt about you
I sang about you
Hell, I **WROTE** about you!
And through all that you couldn't
spare me a second for a quick
response
I wish I could gain the love I see
around me
But I guess I'm not destined for
love
I don't deserve it.

## Boyfriend Contact

If you sign this contract you will..

- ☐ Be loved (conditionally and only at certain times)
- ☐ Never be ignored (if you think hard enough)
- ☐ Not be alone (but you usually will be)
- ☐ Feel happy (only if he talks to you)
- ☐ Never be insecure (except when you are)

Sign here X_________

# Collage

Your face is a collage of people
who have been loved.
Your mother
Your father
Your grandparents
People from hundreds of years ago
have been loved and you are living
proof of that.

# Mosaic

I loved N for 2 years
N did not feel the same way
But he loved rap music
So now I listen to rap music
Just once in a blue moon
But I listen still.

S loved me for one year
I did not feel the same way
So she tried to rape me
So now I think of her every day

I loved C for one year
C did not feel the same way
But he loved hockey
So now I watch hockey
Not often
But sometimes

I loved W for one year
W loved me for about four months
But the distance between us was
too far
And W had someone else
But W loved a small game online

So now I play that small game
online
It's rare
But I still do

I loved B for about six months
B did not love me back
But B loved being weird
So now I love being weird

I "liked" H for one month
H liked me for one month
I did not like H
But H liked a small website
So now I like that small website

I liked R for two weeks
R liked me for two weeks
But the ivory margins on my skin
were ugly to him
But R liked to say he "loafed" me
So I loaf him too

I liked D for one month
D did not like me
But D liked the color green
So now I like the color green

I liked N for two days
N liked me for two days
I didn't have enough time to put
him in my mosaic

I'm not sure how long I liked M
M liked me
Sort of.
He is not in my mosaic
That I know of, at least.

Finally, A.
I loved A for almost one month
A "loved" me for almost one month
But I know he didn't really
But I loved to write
So now A writes

None of me is really **me**.
I am other people, shattered with
loved
And turned into a pretty collage.

## My favorite Stranger

I walk past her
She walks past me
She climbs
I descend
We don't know each other
We're strangers
But I know everything about her.
I know her birthday, her hobbies,
her exes, her dog's name, I know
everything about her
But she's a stranger.
And she knows everything about me
She knows my favorite color is
green
She knows I cry when I get mad
And she knows how I tug the fabric
of my pants around my thighs when
I stand.
She knows I don't like hot drinks
She knows every place I've cut
She knows everyone I've ever loved
But she's a stranger
**I'm**
a stranger.

# I wish

A shooting star passes overhead
and on it, I wish
A four-leaf clover is discovered
in a garden and on it, I wish
A dandelions seeds blow across the
lawn, and on its seeds, I wish
A birthday flame blows out and on
it, I wish
I wish, I wish, I wish
But nothing works.
So when i tiny eyelash falls, I
wish
And when a penny falls into a
fountain, I wish
And even when a wishbone breaks, I
wish
I wish
I wish
I wish.

Beauty is in the eye of the
beholder

Everyone I meet is blind.

## Idiot

Screw up
Fuck up
Dumbass
I can't do anything right
My hand is swollen from cutting my
arm into sushi pieces
FUCK
I messed up
Again.
My friends made a cruel joke and I
laughed
And i feel so bad
But I don't know why what they
said was so bad
I apologized of course
But I'm not sure
I can't cope when people raise
their voices at me
I don't think I'll ever be able to
look at him without remembering
how he got mad
I'm so stupid.

## The shy boy and the idiot

I had a whole scene planned out
I'd ask him about a stupid test I
don't really care about
I'd compliment his outfit and
attempt to start up a conversation
It's like using a wet match.
I wait all day for the perfect
moment to talk to him
It finally reaches
And oh, damn it, I chicken out.
Are we really surprised?
I just want to talk to him
Strike up a weak conversation just
to hear his voice
Just to try
My eyes flicker to him
I think he can feel my eyes on him
It'd be so awkward to even attempt
to talk to him
He's out of my league, definitely
But I can't tell if he's lonely or
just doesn't want to be around
people
I want to help
Does that make me selfish?

I think something is wrong with
me.

# Love Letter

Is it socially acceptable to write
a note to my crush?
Can I scribble out a small
question about him
Or maybe ask about some dumb
chemistry test
Can I write him a little note to
get to know him better?
He seems nice
But what if this goes wrong?
Is it alright for me to write him
a note when words are too
difficult to push out of my mouth?
I second guess everything I say or
do or think
He's quiet
My friends say he's probably more
scared of me than I am of him
But what if he's not?
What if I embarrass myself?

.  .  .

Fuck it

.

# YOUR FAULT!!

It's your fault I can't breathe
properly
Your fault I can't concentrate
Your fault my face is hot
Your fault
Your fault
YOUR FAULT!
And it's your fault I can't stop
thinking of you
If you didn't let me go ahead of
you when it's time to leave class
Or if you didn't politely hand me
my pens when I dropped them
Maybe if you didn't move your feet
when I bent down to take something
out of my bag
Or scurry around if I got near you
This is YOUR FAULT!
And I'm kind of glad

Something as simple as a misclick
in Tetris has the ability to
convince me that I am worthless

You, as a man, do not yet have the
ability to call yourself a father

Let your son do that
Let your daughter do that
Let your child do that
Not you.

I bite and scratch and claw at my
arm
My teacher rambles on about god
knows what
Suddenly I feel something warm
trickle down my arm
Oh fuck
A dark red Jackson Pollock-like
splotch appears on my evergreen
jacket, seeping through the fabric
Oh no
After a few minutes, the amaranth
wine dries
Creating instead a dried-out
cardinal river
No one notices
No one cares
Carefully laid out plans have been
scrapped
I don't know what to do

# Systematic

My plan is ever so carefully laid
out
I walk in
I take my seat
I look to him
And I smile
And I ask about something stupid
that I don't really care about
But as soon as I see him my plan
falters
And shakes
It quakes
And falls apart
Just the sight of this rosey
beauty can throw ever so carefully
laid out plans out the window
Analytic
Systematic
Perfectly attentively planned
And i see him and forget
everything
Hours in advance I scrutinize what
to say to him,
Hours and hours of planning for a
simple hello
And just the fucking sight of him

And i forget everything
Who needs systematic when you have
over the moon, pining, lovelorn,
obsessive, absolutely infatuated
Lovesick Lunar.

# The other man

I throw myself onto my bed and sob
Oh how painful it is when your
delusions prove to be wrong
I guess everything I thought was a
sign was just a series of
coincidences
You were supposed to love me.
ME!
This was supposed to be different,
YOU. were supposed to be different
But no, of course not.
The thoughts in the back of my
head were right
Someone as beautiful as you really
couldn't love someone like me
I hate love
It's stupid and it's painful and
it's only for pretty people
Pretty people like you

Select your character

Female- blonde hair, blue eyes,
skinny, 8/10    character played-
1m times

Female- brown hair, green eyes,
skinny, 9/10    character played-
1.5m times

Female- red hair, brown eyes,
skinny, 7/10    character played-
700,000 times

Trans male- black and purple hair,
brown eyes, fat, 2/10    character
played- ...

# Naked

I want to see you naked
But please keep your clothes on
I want to see you emotionally
naked
I want to know all your secrets
I want to know everything about
you
I can't keep hesitating when
someone asks me your favorite
color
Or how many pets or siblings you
have
I want you to emotionally strip
for me
But keep your clothes ON.

"There are more fish in the sea"

Yeah, but I keep getting stabbed
by the hook
I hate fishing.

# I'm Happy

I am happy
And the sky is green

I am not a crybaby
And the ocean is yellow

I am not anxious
And the trees are purple

I am not alone
And the ground is orange

I am loveable
And the flowers are green

I am sober
And the mountains are red.

# I hate pink

I hate the color pink
The girl who tried to rape me wore
pink
The girl who pushed me off a
diving board wore pink
The expectations for my life were
pink
Her shoes were pink
His jacket is pink
My cheeks glow pink
I hate pink

I was head over heels

I think I have a concussion

# Beg

Never let me beg the way I begged
those nights
I tried to justify his lack of
response
Reason after reason, only slightly
realistic
And even if they were the truth,
they'd still be unreasonable.
My attempts to understand his
departure were pathetic
I was desperate
I still miss him
I miss his pretty hair
And his pretty clothes
And the way we talked alone
But I'm better without him, right?
I hope so.

A life without love is tragic

Yet a tragedy is nothing without
love

For love is the greatest tragedy
of all

If loving you was a sin
I'd be in hell tenfold

You break me like you break your
promises
Harshly
Painfully
And far too often

A writer without tragedy is not a
writer
They are a person with ideas that
are bottled up with a wine cork
and nowhere to go.

## The Center of the Universe

Scientifically, there is no real
center of the universe
I, however, disagree.
The center of the universe is
relative
If I stand here before you and
grasp your hands in mine
And I look into your hazel eyes
And when I speak, I tell you that
you are the center of the
universe,
It's relative
If I speak these words I truly
mean them
You are indeed, the center of the
universe
For me at least
However, this is temporary
Love is not science
It is not permanent
Not for someone like me
So when you stand before me
And the words you speak show that
I am not yours and you are not
mine

The center of the universe is not
you anymore
Maybe it is for someone else
But not me
When I speak and say that you are
the center of the universe, don't
believe me.
For this is true only until it
isn't
For truth is relative
And so is love
And so are you.


Small little fuck-ups


Small little fuckups
Every other day

Small little fuckups
Leave my life at bay
I cannot speak
Cannot dream
Cannot sip on my drink
For these small little fuckups
Get in my way.
I open a wrapper too loudly in a
quiet room
I turn in a paper too early
My breasts are too big
My stomach is too large
My height is impaired
Small little fuckups
I don't dare to fix.

The universe is a child with Legos

It snaps people together just to
later bring them apart




Rosewood Tree


Large, calloused, roots
2 Achey, chubby trunks
Overused rosewood waist

2 chubby, fat-filled branches
Leaves the color of coal
Apples the shade of dirt
Lichens dance upon the core
He is a short and stout sapling
And he is soon to wither.

Every story was, at one point,
untold
Some have just been held in for so
long it's revolutionary when it's
released

If he wanted to
He would.

Dear depression,

Fuck you.

Sincerely, lunar

Leaving

I'm leaving
I'm leaving this school
I'm leaving for a hopefully better
place

Although, let's be honest, it'll
be worse.
I'm going to leave every single
one of my friends
Every single one of my enemies
I'll start anew
Maybe I won't be lunar anymore
Maybe I'll be Max
Or Cora
Aurora
Maybe Kai
Who knows
Maybe, maybe, maybe
I'll be a new person
With a new start
I'll be a pencil on a blank sheet
of paper

I'm the main character, you don't
need to save me

Kindness isn't enough to survive
as a teenager

Contrapasso

Contrapasso

The idea that your punishment in
Hell reflects your wrongdoings in
life
If my sin is suicide will I be
sentenced to cut myself for all
eternity?
Cut
Cut
Cut
Cut until my arm falls off
Would I even hate it?
Would I revel in my suicidal hell
for all eternity?

I'm a good person
I'm a good person
I'm a good person

I'm a good person
I'm a good person
I'm a good person
I'm a good person
I'm a good person
I'm a good person
I'm a good person
I'm a good person
I'm a good person
I'm a good person
I'm a good person
I'm a good person
I'm a good person
I'm a good person
I'm a good person
I'm a good person
I'm a good person
I'm a good person
I'm a good person
I'm a good person
I'm a good person
I'm a good person
I'm a good person
I swear.

# Good things, Bad people

"Why do bad things happen to good
people?"
I don't bother myself with such
trivial questions
For I know that there is no such
thing as a good person
Instead, I ask why good things
happen to bad people.
I watch the people who bully me
smile and have the love I so
desire.
God, do you know how much that
pains me?
I'm an okay person!
I'm not good but I'm okay..
I guess.
But I'm not as bad as they are
So why do they get the one thing I
want in life
They Are full and fed and I starve
This isn't fair.

## Emotional

My emotions are a broken faucet
When I want to cry I cannot
When I tilt my head up and do
everything in my power to not cry
I sob
Wail
Cry
Kick
Scream
SOMEONE CALL THE PLUMBER!

Violets bloom as scars on my skin

Anxiety creeps up like a tiger on
the prowl in the zoo of my mind

My evil thoughts howl in my head

My mind is a chaotic jungle

I'm cheating on my promise to stay
sober


I wish I were more faithful

## One Star

My book has received its very
first rating
One star.
My book is horrible
My heart
My soul
My thoughts
Are horrible.
And yes, I am aware they are a
troll
I am aware they've never read my
book but I put my everything into
these poems
These poems are my heart
My soul
My thoughts
My everything
You can't just say that and expect
nothing to happen to you even
though nothing will
I know it's wrong to write about
this woman who feeds off of my
cries and sobs but it *hurts*
It is a bullet in my heart when
you insult my life source
My heart

My soul
My thoughts
My legacy.
These poems are my legacy,
A legacy no one might read
As I write this now I realize when
I die these poems will be all I'll
have left to tell my story, the
story of who I am
Who I was.
Maybe historians will read my soul
and praise who I was long after my
death
Or maybe I'm just a "deluded,
overprivileged "girl"
We'll find out in a hundred years
I suppose
Lunar Patni
Signing off




For now..

## Another Silly Crush

I want to be the reason you wake
up in the mornings
I want you to come to school and
count down the minutes until you
see me
I want you to wait for me to text
you and smile when I finally work
up the courage
I want you to fantasize about
stupid scenarios with a dumb grin
on your face and wish they would
come true
Seek me out, brush your hand
against mine and blush,
romanticize every interaction we
have
Draw hearts on every paper "W+L"
Long for us to be together every
day, every second
Pray to anyone you believe in for
me to love you back, even for a
fraction of a second, just a
percent of how you love me.
Write about me like a fool
Love me and love me and love me.
Be clingy and adore me

Beg for me like I do you
Please.

# Circus freak

A new insecurity has been gained
Sagging breasts.
My mother constantly criticizes my
breasts and now I can't go
anywhere without trying to fix
them
They sag with the severity of a
dented roof
Ugliness flows through my veins
like blood and everyone knows it
Point and laugh!
Point and laugh at the ugly freak!
My school is a circus and I am a
freak.

# Ratings

Transphobic characters scribble
messy ratings on my soul
"Privileged ranting"
"Boring"
"Repetitive"
"Delusional teenage "girl"
My work is so bad they can't even
qualify it as real poetry
Or as they say, "poetry".
"Save yourself and never read
this!"
"Derivative"
"Schitzo ramblings"
"Wouldn't recommend to my worst
enemy"
"narcissistic"
"Unreliable narrator", they call
me
But I am proud of my work.
My poetry is delicately crafted
and intricately woven.
Poe was hated until he died
And so were Frost and Dickens and
Angeleo.
Every great poet is hated,
therefore I thank you

Thank you for helping me start my
bridge to fame.

## Boiling Alive

Red-hot anger seeps through my
veins
They talk about me while I'm right
there
I can hear you!
But it's like I'm not even there
I'm on fire and I can see red
Boiling shades of scarlet cloud my
mind
Stop talking about me!
And it takes everything in my
power to not stand up and slap him
square across the face
God, I hate him.
The most conceded being alive
chooses to bully me relentlessly
My career is ruined
And I am boiling alive in my
anger.

FATTY

When I walk down the halls, the
ground shakes
Thud
Thud
Thud.
Birds squeak overhead
FATTY!
FATTY!
FATTY!
I lower myself onto the school
desks
Creak
Creak
Creak
I'm so fat the desk can't even
hold me
People laugh at me and cackle
FATASS
FATASS
FATASS!
My parents constantly speak about
their weight and my diet
I wish I was deaf
I can't do anything right
Especially lose weight.

From Lunar
To {}

Dear {},

I hate you.
No really, I hate you now.
I always love to think about how I
might wake up someday and still be
friends
Not anymore.
My career
My life
My legacy
RUINED.
Because of you
God, I hate you.
I hate you
I hate you
I HATE YOU!!!
I want things to happen to you
that I've never wanted to happen
to people before.
I can't believe for the life of me
that I loved you
I can't believe I still miss you
I hate you from the bottom of my
heart

So from the absolute deepest
depths of my soul

Fuck you.

Sincerely, Lunar

## Hitman

I had a hit hired on me
Normally I'd use this as a
metaphor because, really, what
high school boy has a hit hired on
him?
Me.
She goes around looking to hire a
friend to hurt, beat, or kill me
I wrote a will
I was so scared
I was so alone
Not a single soul believed me.
And even if you didn't believe me,
not a single soul comforted me.
My closest friends let me cry and
wail and fully believe my life was
to end
Naive lunar
Stupid lunar
IDIOT LUNAR!!

I am drunk on literature

## Polaroid

Our friendship is nothing but an
old Polaroid now

An old photo-booth-photo that is
creased and hung on the wall of
your room right above your bed

You can sleep with me watching
over you, not a hint of malice in
my gaze

Once we get back to classes you'll
see anger and hatred in my eyes

And you deserve it

But I miss you
I really do.

I still have half of our Polaroid

Blue eyes were always my least
favorite


Until I met you.

Maybe that's all I'll ever be

A once upon a time with no happily
ever after

A prologue without an epilogue

A book that ends on an odd page

A novel with a cliffhanger

A beginning without an

You're gone

But you're everywhere
You're not here
But you're *here*
You're not next to me
But I can't get rid of you
You won't leave
But you couldn't stay.

Why can't you love me like the
boys I hate do?

I sit curled up on the bathroom
floor
Bloody blade in my hand
Wine dripping down my arm
*How to never stop being sad*
playing in the background
Praying
Hoping
Wishing
Begging for me to die

## Nonverbal

A spider web coats my lips
I can't open them
They are stapled shut
Why
Why
Why can't I speak
Does it even matter?
No one speaks to me.

# Her

The knife twists when I see you
talking to her
You "can't" talk to me
But you have no issue speaking
with her
And fuck.
Thinking of you makes me look like
a fool in my classes
I freeze up
God, where's a pause button when I
need it
I'm supposed to be over you, damn
it!
But thoughts of being stabbed in
the heart
Bleeding out everywhere
Falling backward and you catching
me
Holding me in your arms as I
wither
I know it's wrong but the thought
of you holding me as I die clouds
my thoughts
I want to spend my final moments
with you

Even though I know you'll spend
them with her

You are a lighter
I am a candle
We had a spark
Now I am burned out

I have the ability to save the
world
Or to destroy it

Oh, what to choose?

Alone in a room full of people

Loved ten thousand miles away from
you

I never have the option to be
wrapped in someone's arms when I'm
drowning in a sea of tragedy
I don't have a lifeboat of love
Im alone
Of course
As always

# I don't feel so good

I don't feel so good
Not in my stomach
Instead in my head
I feel like harming myself but no
one would care
I sit alone here, the seats beside
me are bare
I long to be liked.
I hate being alone
But I'm so used to it
I might as well call it home

## Alone

I spend my days increasingly more
alone than the last
A boy deliberately moved to stay
away from me
A girl looked at me out of the
corner of her eye, disgust filling
her view
Alone and disgusting
Maybe I'm a disease
People must stay at least 20 feet
away from me
Or maybe I'm just a boy
A boy who's different.

# Infected

"Don't sit by 'her' you'll get
infected"
Yes, I'm disgusting.
But what exactly would you get
infected with?
Would I, on contact, make you as
weird as me?
As queer as me?
As never insincere as me?
What *exactly* are you worried
about?
Ugliness isn't contagious
Only on the inside.
And my weight isn't infectious
My scars won't harm you
So what are you really afraid of?

# Ash, my love

A boy named blanket cuddles my
lover every night
A girl named pillow holds up his
head
People named clothes touch him
all-day
Twins named shoes massage his feet
He stares at girls named books day
and night
He holds hands with a boy named
pencil
And yet he's still loyal
And he still chose me.

## Chemically Tired

Whilst you are in the company of
the being you are closest to, you
might get tired.
This is due to the art of love.
Dopamine flows through your head
like love out of my heart.
Chemically bonded with my partner.
Oh, love.

# Cry

There is a bulge in my throat
bigger than the one in your pants.
That's not really saying much
though, is it?
I want to cry so bad, but I've
been doing so well.
Well… one tear won't do anything,
right?
One tear… oh.

Love me like you love my brother

PART TWO


POEMS FOR DH

Drew [redacted] never did, never had, or never will love me.

## Like a Psychic

Trace my palm like a psychic
Rub my back like a masseuse
Pretend to love me like a
prostitute
Talk to me like a hotline worker
Build me up like a construction
worker
Tear me down like a demolitions
expert
As long as I'm with you

One-sided love

Our love is one-sided
Like this poem

I want you to look for me the way
I look for you

I want you to bask in my unseen
beauty the way I do yours

I want you to long to touch my
hair and go on stupid dates and
hold me close the way I wish for
you

I want the feeling of unrequited
love to eat at you like a termite
as it does me

I want you.

I want you and only you

I want you for the rest of
eternity

If an asteroid were to hit the
earth in 5 minutes and I called to
say I love you, would you pick up?

There is no way to love someone
into loving you back.

You are my future
You are my sky, my stars, my night
and day
You are the flowers that bloom
every spring
You are the burst of happiness I
feel when I see an angel number
You are my future
And I'm not even your present.

Loving you is my favorite way to
destroy myself

I understand why you don't love me

How could you love me when I don't
even love myself?

## Those eyes of yours

God, those coffee eyes.
Or were they hazel?
Amber
Maybe azure
Maybe they were stormy like your
personality
Maybe they were emerald
I'm not sure
I never got close enough to see
But I still love them
And i still love you
Those eyes of yours
Whatever color they are, they
still pierce my soul
They're so beautiful

I never stood a chance.

I got my heart broken by a love
that never even happened

He never left my mind
Always haunting me
Clouding my mind
All I could ever think about

I never even entered his

What are you thinking about?
I know I'm thinking of you
Again.
But are you thinking of someone
else?

The only love that lasts is the
one in art

A strand of your hair could bring
the universe to its knees to pray
for your forgiveness

You look happier without me.

Maybe it's for the best

I love you, D.
I love you unconditionally
I love your pimples
I love the knots in your hair
I love the veins in your arms
I love your pale ghostlike skin
I even love the way you ignore me
I love the way you are cold to me
I love the way you hate me
Because no matter how much it
hurts, it's still you
And I love you.

The way you drew on my soul was
stronger than a Sharpie

You're not mine

But I can't bear to lose you

# L'amour de ma vie

Kiss me on my forehead and take me
to see the stars

I so badly want to know what you
think of me

I can't do this yet.

I'll wait

I love you today
I love you tomorrow
I love you the day after and the
next

I love you for months
For years
For as long as I can
For as long as you need me to

If I were to live a century more
I'd love you all the while

You belong in a museum

I wonder if you ever think of me
when you can't sleep at 3 am

For you, I'd kneel down in front
of a priest, bloody hands and
laughing and knowing that for you,
I'd do it all again

The sound of rain
The smell of grass
The grainy sand
The smooth pebbles
The light of the sun
The beams of the moon
All lead me
Back to you

I hope we look up at the same star
each night and wish for each other

And I hope the moon smiles down on
us both and whispers,
"Soon my dears"

I hope you find this
I hope you read this

Lead me on


I wrote over twenty poems about
you in one day
On the same day, I got my wish
I found out what you really think
of me
I'm a pity case, is that it?
I know you don't really care about
the deluded "girl" who follows you
around, but god.
Why'd you have to lead me on?

As the waves kiss the shore, let
me kiss your soul

Maybe one day there will be a "you
and me"

There is no way we only met by accident. People don't meet by accident

Let me take you to a New York City rooftop, let us lie on our backs, and let me point out every constellation I know, every star I see.

I think my heart was doomed to be
shattered the moment our eyes met

There are no fairy tales for fat
boys

I think it's okay that I fell for
you

I think hoping was what brought my
downfall

I didn't want this to be another
lesson

I wish it could been you

I wish it could been here

I wish it could been now

But its not

And it wasn't

Cry until you can't anymore

Love is the greatest tragedy

I'm not going to let you take off
my shirt, even if you use the
gentleness of one thousand
butterflies

I'm not pretty enough to be asked
to 'just go to the bathroom'

But I'm pretty enough to be sent
things I definitely do not want to
see

How do I answer when you ask me
why I'm sad and the answer is you?

It doesn't matter, you won't ask
me anyway

Let me be your devoted servant and
write your name in the stars

I don't care if you break my bones

As long as you don't break my
heart

The only time i'll get flowers is
at my funeral

I hope you drown in the sea of
tears you've caused

Everyone saw it coming but me

And i so desperately wanted us to
prove them wrong

You are not mine to lose

I'd rather taste you than caviar

Id hold your hands even soaked in
my own blood

Maybe this is hell

My world is shaking around me
Walls come crumbling down
Windows shatter
Doors crash
I'm in the eye of the hurricane
It's not quite here.

If only

Your love is like quicksand

I'm stuck

Sick


You're sick
You threw up in the bathroom at
work
And now I'm worried.
I'm not supposed to worry about
you anymore
I'm supposed to be over you
But you threw up
You're sick
My baby that isn't really mine is
sick
And i feel terrible because i
can't comfort you
I'll see you later today
And suddenly, writing this gives
me such a strong sense of deja vu.
You're sick
And i'm so worried
So i went to the bathroom
And i threw up

If you had to ask if i had a crush
on you,

Surely that means you were
thinking about me?

I wish i were her

## Gone for Good

Are you gone for good now?
I ask around about you
And i tell my friends i'll send
one final text to you
If you dont reply the next day ill
be done with you
This should be easy.
But it's the next day and my
feelings for you haven't faded yet
But you should be gone
I need to rid you of my mind
Get out get out get out
But you stay
Just in my mind
Really, you couldn't care enough
to stay.

I wish you sweet dreams

Even though wishing you will only
give me sour ones.

I want to feel love like everyone
else does

I need to stop writing about you

I look around and it's all you

I tried so hard to let it be you

You tried so hard to guarantee i t
wasnt me

## Goodbye, Drew

This is the last poem i will
(hopefully) ever write about Drew
[REDACTED]
I dont think i'm over you yet
But I know I can try.
You're bad for me
You don't care about me
You've made that blatantly obvious
I need to stop
So for my own health, i have faith in
myself that this will be the last poem
i write about you
I dont think its love
I don't think it ever was
But if you see this, drew,
I like you.
I like you alot
And i hate you
And i wish you made a move
And i wish you felt the same way
And i wish you were kinder to me
I wish you'd tell me what i did wrong
But it's not your fault.
Mostly.
Goodbye, drew
Hopefully forever.

PART THREE

Please god, i am not your
strongest soldier

Why do people always look at me
that way

I'm the only one not in a group

The only one sitting alone

I go to work everyday hoping
you'll be there

You go to work every day hoping i
won't

I wanted to be in love so bad i
convinced myself i could taste
your lips when you're not even a
real person

We're friends now

But it's more like

You're my friend

And i'm not yours

Love isn't supposed to hurt

You put so much effort into loving
that when someone doesn't, you
feel they dont love you back.

I want to be good for my age

I need to yell so loud you could
hear me even with you ignoring me

I was supposed to stop writing
about you

Id carve your name into my skin
and the stars

Your arm brushed mine
And you probably don't even
remember it
But it burned
And it felt like a forest of hairs
stood up on my skin

All the grains of sand on the
shores
All the stars in the sky
All the bubbles in a bathtub

And i still love you more

I didn't want to wake up

I can still feel her hands on me

Her eyes on my chest

Her mouth drooling at the sight of
me

And for once, i was pretty

My heart breaks every time i see
you, baby

I need to stop searching for
forever in the temporary

And so do you, reader.

Your final breath was mine too

We were supposed to go back to
normal

Red

Red is love
Red is lust
Red is romance
Red is passion

                    Red is power
                   Red is murder
                    Red is blood
                     Red is pain

You showed me both sides of red

www.ingramcontent.com/pod-product-compliance
Lightning Source LLC
Chambersburg PA
CBHW020329160726
47992CB00004B/1765